Welc

NAOMI STARKEY

Are you afraid of the dark? Even if we no longer literally fear the night time and have to sleep with a light on, most of us will shrink from the idea of spiritual darkness, the 'dark night of the soul'. Although we know God promises to be with us through all kinds of 'night', the thought does not stop us from being fearful at the prospect of experiencing a dark time ourselves.

And who has not woken unexpectedly in the night and then spent hours awake, watching the numbers on the clock and longing for a morning that seems to take forever to arrive? Might it in fact be the case that our Father is waiting for us to turn to him, to be open to what he might say to us, at a time when there are no other distractions and when we are perfectly still?

In the opening article of this issue, Celia Bowring writes movingly of encountering God 'in the night', and how her own experience of unexpected, debilitating illness tested the extent to which she was really willing to trust him. The idea of praying 'through the night' is picked up in a different way by Andy Freeman, who shares some of the story of the 24–7 Prayer movement. In just a few years, it has spread around the world, catching the imaginations of young people in particular and encouraging them to wait on God.

We also feature, among other articles, the work of St Michael's Convent in Ham, Surrey, Burrswood Hospital, and a saint who is mostly remembered now in connection with what he gets up to on one particular night of the year—St Nicholas!

Naomi Starkey

1

Text copyright © BRF 2008
Authors retain copyright in their own work
Illustrations copyright © Ian Mitchell, Ray and Corinne Burrows, 2008

Published by
The Bible Reading Fellowship
15 The Chambers, Vineyard
Abingdon, OX14 3FE
United Kingdom
Tel: +44 (0)1865 319700
Email: enquiries@brf.org.uk
Website: www.brf.org.uk

ISBN 978 1 84101 542 2
First published 2008
10 9 8 7 6 5 4 3 2 1 0

Acknowledgments
Scripture quotations taken from The New Revised Standard Version of the Bible, Anglicized Edition, copyright © 1989, 1995 by the Division of Christian Education of the National Council of the Churches of Christ in the USA, are used by permission. All rights reserved.

Scripture quotations taken from The Holy Bible, New International Version, copyright © 1973, 1978, 1984 by International Bible Society, are used by permission of Hodder & Stoughton, a division of Hodder Headline Ltd. All rights reserved. 'NIV' is a registered trademark of International Bible Society. UK trademark number 1448790.

Scripture quotations taken from The Holy Bible, Today's New International Version. Copyright © 2004 by International Bible Society. Used by permission of Hodder & Stoughton, a division of Hodder Headline Ltd. All rights reserved. 'TNIV' is a registered trademark of International Bible Society.

Extracts from The Book of Common Prayer of 1662, the rights of which are vested in the Crown in perpetuity within the United Kingdom, are reproduced by permission of Cambridge University Press, Her Majesty's Printers.

A catalogue record for this book is available from the British Library

Printed by Gutenberg Press, Tarxien, Malta

Quiet Spaces

VOLUME 12

CONTENTS

Trusting God
in the night

Celia Bowring is prayer coordinator for CARE (Christian Action Research and Education), which brings Christian insight and experience to matters of public policy and practical caring and educational initiatives. She is married to Lyndon, who is CARE's chairman, and they have three grown-up children. Celia writes and speaks on a range of subjects, *including prayer, and most recently wrote 'We're In This Together' (Authentic, 2005) for women married to Christian leaders.*

Perhaps like me you enjoy lying awake in the darkness sometimes, thinking and praying about people and situations that come to mind. Night is part of the rhythm of our lives, created by God who declared it to be good. Its darkness provides the best atmosphere for rest, quietness and the sleep needed so that the body's systems can recuperate.

However, night can also be a dark, lonely and even fearful time as physical pain, distress, anxiety or 'life overload' closes in—especially in the small hours when we are at our most vulnerable. And as well as literal nights we may sometimes pass through life experiences like the 'darkest valley' referred to in Psalm 23.

Maybe we only really discover the depths of God's faithfulness and compassionate love for us in our 'night experiences'. Christian believers throughout the centuries have confirmed this to be so—that at certain times God lets us walk through some very dark places for his own good, though often mysterious, purposes. Along with other New Testament writers, James writes about such trials in positive terms: 'Consider it pure joy… the testing of your faith produces perseverance. Let perseverance finish its work so that you may be mature and complete, not lacking anything' (James 1:2–4, TNIV). In Isaiah 45:3, God promises 'treasures of darkness, riches stored in secret places'. In the book of Job, Elihu laments that no one calls to 'God my Maker, who gives songs in the night' (Job 35:10) and one unknown writer has observed, 'We can only appreciate the miracle of a sunrise if we have waited in darkness.'

This promise of dawn gives us the hope we need in the dead of night and the last chapters of the Bible describe the ultimate sunrise of heaven for those who belong to Christ: 'There will be no more night.

Many people believe that death is the end and that there is no hope beyond the grave

This promise of dawn gives us the hope we need in the dead of night

They will not need the light of a lamp or the light of the sun, for the Lord God will give them light. And they will reign for ever and ever' (Revelation 22:5). No uncertainties, no fears, no pain—but completeness, love and joy.

Not everyone believes this, and talking about death has become a taboo subject in our time, even though it is the one and only certainty we can have about our life and perhaps the most important subject we could consider. Many people believe that death is the end and that there is no hope beyond the grave. The Welsh writer Dylan Thomas (1914–53) wrote his most famous poem, 'Do not go gentle into that good night', following his father's death, as a passionate recognition of human frailty and hopelessness in the face of that 'dying of the light'.

Do not go gentle into that good night,
Old age should burn and rave at close of day;
Rage, rage against the dying of the light.

Were all the hopes for humanity **doomed to an eternal night?**

Death is described in the Bible as 'the last enemy' (1 Corinthians 15:26). Anyone who has been bereaved is familiar with the deep grief it brings. Those who know they have little time left to live may seriously consider just what they believe will happen when they die. If we do not believe in the resurrection, wrote Paul to the Corinthian church, 'if only for this life we have hope in Christ, we are to be pitied more than all others' (1 Corinthians 15:19). Without God's glorious promise of eternity in his presence, our lives are meaningless.

The truth at the very heart of our Christian faith is that God has 'rescued us from the dominion of darkness and brought us into the kingdom of the Son he loves, in whom we have redemption, the forgiveness of sins' (Colossians 1:13–14). Although no match for the Almighty God, the power and the evil intent of the devil are a reality and Calvary was where the decisive battle between light and darkness took place. As Jesus died on the cross, Luke's Gospel says that darkness fell over the whole land, as if the day had been swallowed up. Had the Light of the world been snuffed out? Were all the hopes for humanity doomed to an eternal night? Evil might have thought it had triumphed but two days later, every shadow of sadness, all the darkness of sin and even death itself were put to flight as Easter Day dawned and Christ rose victoriously from the grave.

Today we are between the two comings of Christ; believing, rescued and redeemed and with his Spirit living in us but not yet in heaven, free from the effects of sin and the influence of 'the powers of this dark world' (Ephesians 6:12). We are imperfect people shining as brightly as we can, sharing in the sufferings of humanity in a benighted world. Sometimes we will be called upon to be tested and even to go through what some have described as 'the dark night of the soul' when nothing seems to make sense and God feels far away—a personal physical, emotional, mental

and spiritual time of darkness.

The Gospels tell us that, before he died in that noonday gloom, Jesus suffered his 'dark night' alone in Gethsemane. His friends dozed among the olive trees, leaving him alone to face the most terrifying hour of his life so far. Luke describes how Christ 'knelt down and prayed, "Father, if you are willing, take this cup from me; yet not my will, but

> **...believing, rescued and redeemed** and with his Spirit living in us but not yet in heaven

All he can do is to hold on to what he believes about God

yours be done." An angel from heaven appeared to him and strengthened him. And being in anguish, he prayed more earnestly, and his sweat was like drops of blood falling to the ground' (Luke 22:41–44). After that, Jesus courageously went forward to fulfil the lonely and agonizing destiny God had planned to save the human race. Nobody has ever endured a worse

night than he did. Jesus really understands how we feel in our darkest moments and walks with us, even though we may not have any clear indication that he's there.

Job was a godly man with a wonderful life. The Bible describes him as 'the greatest man among all the people of the East' (Job 1:3), rich, respected and religious—until one dreadful day, without any warning at all, his world caved in and he lost absolutely everything: property, livestock and even family. Job responded humbly to this disastrous turn of events and worshipped God, acknowledging that nothing had ever truly belonged to him anyway. Later he was afflicted with a painful skin disease and, as he sat dejected in a pile of ashes, his wife urged him to turn his back on the God who had let them down so badly. But Job stayed faithful, saying, 'Shall we accept good from God, and not trouble?' (2:10). He was tested for a long time, kept in the dark and isolated in his anguished search to understand why God had allowed this to happen. Job experienced his 'dark night of the soul' but eventually lived to tell his remarkable tale of discovering what God was really like, meeting him in the midst of his doubt and depression. If none of the bad things had ever happened, Job would have missed this.

The book of Job uniquely takes us behind the scenes to see what is happening in the spiritual realms—an encounter between the Almighty and the devil. Unlike us, Job is totally unaware that God and Satan are debating the depth of his devotion to his Maker and Lord. All he can do is to hold on to what he believes about God, be honest about his confusion and wait for answers. Like Job, our human perspective on life is severely limited and in the dark times we must learn to 'live by faith, not by sight' (2 Corinthians 5:7). Often it is when we find ourselves in the dark that we discover what we really believe. The question to ask is not so much 'Why is this happening?' but 'How does God want me to respond to this—and will I trust him whatever happens?'

Ten years ago I went through a physical and emotional experience that put these truths to the test for me. One day I was energetically involved with various projects, running a busy household and organizing three school-aged children—and the next I couldn't walk or use my hands properly and felt as if I had been thrown aside like a rag doll. I was diagnosed with multiple sclerosis, the very name of which drove an arrow of terror into me. In some ways it was even worse for my husband Lyndon than for me. What lay ahead? Would I be like this forever, or get much worse? There was so much unknown; everyday living was a challenge and for months I felt too weak to do anything at all—including pray. I had hoped to scale new heights of spirituality through my ordeal, but that seemed to be impossible. Once, feeling rather panicky inside the

claustrophobic tube of a scanning machine, I could not summon up a single verse of scripture to comfort me—even Psalm 23 eluded me! All I had left was to cry out in the depths of my being the name, 'Jesus!'

I recovered, gradually at first. Then after a couple of years I progressed well enough to cancel my Disabled Living Allowance and even my very useful disability parking badge! I thank God for his mercy towards me, the wonderful support of other people's prayers and practical love, and the ongoing strength I have

One day I was energetically involved

with various projects... and the next I couldn't walk

enjoyed since then. Compared with many people my 'night' was not a severe one, although I found it pretty horrible. Did anything positive come out of it? Oh yes! I would not have missed it for anything. I learned to treasure simple blessings and began to realize that even when I can't *do* anything I am so precious to God. Sometimes it is in our weakest moments that he works most powerfully within us.

Thankfully I escaped the depression that many endure, including some remarkable and gifted Christian

9

people. The night experience of mental illness really is a dark one. Following his daughter's death, Martin Luther suffered from it and Florence Nightingale had bad bouts of depression all her life. William Cowper, a devout Christian writer who lived in the 18th century, was

...the full extent of the treasure God created in the darkness of his life

> One day everything that is hidden will be brought to light, **all injustice will be righted...**

another. He lived in Olney, where Reverend John Newton, the converted slave ship captain, was vicar. Newton cared for him and whenever Cowper was threatened with an attack of depression he suggested they work together to provide hymns for the weekly meetings.

This gesture of friendship not only helped Cowper but resulted in the writing of many wonderful hymns which still give much encouragement and incentive to worship 200 years

later, all over the world. Cowper sometimes led prayer meetings and also poured out his life in practical ways. Newton's testimony of him was this: 'He loved the poor. He often visited them in their cottages, conversed with them, counselled and comforted them in their distresses; and those who were seriously disposed were often cheered and animated by his prayers.' In the end this dear man who struggled to be a light in the darkness of his almost unbearable mental torment actually died in a state of despair. Newton wrote of his death, 'Sometimes God puts his children to bed in the dark.' But in heaven William Cowper, along with us all, will see the full extent of the treasure God created in the darkness of his life.

What can we do when we find ourselves in a 'night season'? I believe it all comes back to one simple question—do we trust God? Jesus in Gethsemane wished his future was different but submitted to God's will. Job, fearing his life was about to end, affirmed his faith in a good God, saying: 'Though he slay me, yet will I hope in him' (Job 13:15). Even if everything is dark and we cannot see or understand what God is doing, we can still choose to cling immovably to him with a trust that cannot be shaken. One day everything that is hidden will be brought to light, all injustice will be righted and every sacrifice of faith will be rewarded.

One day darkness will be no more and light and life will really begin. ∎

Labyrinths and
prayer journeys

Ian Tarrant is Coordinating Christian Chaplain at the University of Nottingham. He co-authored 'Labyrinths and Prayer Stations' (Grove, 2004).

Have you ever found it helpful to walk as you pray? Perhaps in 'quiet places', like beaches, forests or hilltops, or a shopping street late at night, when the shoppers have gone home? Or perhaps there are times when you pray in the hustle and bustle of a high street or railway station? Have you prayed while cooking, gardening or drawing? While looking through old Christmas

Perhaps there are times when you pray in the hustle and bustle of a high street

cards or the daily paper?

There are times when it is good to follow the exhortation of Psalm 46, to 'be still, and know that I am God' (v. 10, NIV)—but we are creatures of movement and activity, and we can all encounter God as we

Diagram 1

Diagram 2

walk and as we do. We expect our encounters with God to transform us at a variety of levels. Movement and action do not just symbolize that transformation—they open the warp and woof of our being, and allow the Holy Spirit to enter.

Labyrinths

Archeological evidence shows that human beings have made labyrinths since prehistoric times, though we can only guess at their purpose. By the word 'labyrinth' I mean a path

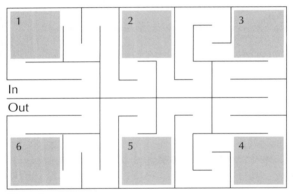

Diagram 3

that turns around itself, without branches, ending at a 'central' point or leading back to the outside world. You cannot get lost in a labyrinth! (For a path with branches, where you can get lost, many prefer the term 'maze'.)

Christians have used

labyrinths marked on the ground since the first few centuries of the faith, although again we are not sure exactly how. We do know, however, that by the Middle Ages people would walk a labyrinth to meditate and pray and that some saw this as a substitute for a pilgrimage to the Holy Land.

Walking a labyrinth is not to be rushed. The walker should see it not as a ritual to complete but as an open-ended encounter with God, and allow time for a gentle journey in, some stillness at the centre and an unhurried return to the outside world. While it is possible for more than one person to walk a labyrinth at the same time, they should enter it at suitable intervals, and it should never become crowded.

The journey inwards can be a time for letting go of worldly concerns and placing them into the hands of God. Choosing to follow the path of the labyrinth, often marked out on the floor, rather than with walls that force compliance, symbolizes freely choosing to follow the way of Christ. As we walk, our distance from the centre varies, and we do not know how soon the goal will be reached—another parallel with the spiritual life. The walls of the labyrinth, real or imagined, separate us from the world outside, giving both security and detachment.

Time at the centre can be spent in reflection and prayer, perhaps using scripture or some other aid.

The journey outwards can be a time for thanksgiving and praise for the encounter in the stillness, and for committing ourselves afresh to God and picking up once more the responsibilities that God wants us to assume. Ideally we return to the world refreshed and renewed for service.

Find one... or make your own

You may find a labyrinth that you can use like this in a cathedral, public park or stately home, close to where you live, or when you are on holiday. Try searching on the Internet, but beware of disappointment! Gilbert Scott's pavement labyrinth in Ely Cathedral is near the main entrance and serves as a busy thoroughfare, so is not a good place for quiet reflection. The labyrinth in Chartres Cathedral often has rows of chairs across it. The one at Norwich Cathedral, however, is made of stones set in the grass of a quiet cloistered courtyard and is accessible whenever the cathedral is open.

You may want to make your own labyrinth, either as a temporary facility or to be a permanent feature in a building or grounds. On a beach you can draw a labyrinth in the sand with a stick. You can lay one out with rope, ribbon or marking tape

> Time at the centre can be spent in reflection and prayer

on any firm flat surface. In a garden you might use rocks or paving stones. Nevertheless, be sure to plan it on paper before you commit money, materials or time.

Various plans of labyrinths can be found on the Internet, and if you want to use the classical 'Cretan' design (diagram 1) there is an easy procedure for drawing it, starting with the central cross. You can, of course, also design your own. (Diagram 2 is my own—copy at will!)

Make best use of the space available, but don't cramp the walkers. Be sure that there is space at the centre to pause and reflect, perhaps for more than one person, if you anticipate a number of people using your labyrinth at the same time. The Chartres labyrinth has a flower-shaped centre, providing space for six people to be still. Make the path wide enough. Will people need to pass one another? Will somebody in a wheelchair be visiting?

An opportunity for an individual to be still before God and be **transformed by his Spirit**

A path that turns around itself

Stations

Many Christians will be familiar with the Stations of the Cross, used to help the faithful reflect on Jesus' suffering and death. Images or sculptures represent a number of stages in the Passion story, and groups or individuals may visit these in order, using an appropriate text and prayer at each one. The number and content of the stations has varied over the centuries. The recent Church of England resource book *Common Worship: Times and Seasons* (Church House Publishing, 2006) gives 14 stations, all scripture-based, with a text and prayer for each. The same book gives material also for 14 Stations of the Resurrection.

This idea of following a story or a theme through a series of stations can be combined with the labyrinth concept. This was famously done in St Paul's Cathedral, London, in March 2000. This labyrinth has since toured the country, and materials are available so that you can reproduce it for your own community. For photos and full details see the website www.labyrinth.org.uk.

Again, you can design your own, following a narrative in the Bible or developing an ordered sequence of themes, for example as in the Lord's Prayer. The path needs to have both an entrance and an exit, so that each station is visited only once. Diagram 3 (p. 12) shows how you could lay out a labyrinth in a rectangular space (such as a church hall), with six stations for prayer.

Ideally the stations will be more than a picture to look at or a text to read. Just as walking the labyrinth engages the body as well as the mind, stations can be made to engage other senses and muscles. For example, the first station in a labyrinth based on the story of Noah and the flood might offer newspapers (local and national), scissors and a pin board, with a text like this...

The wickedness of humanity: read Genesis 6:11–13 [include text for those without Bibles to hand]...

Cut out a newspaper story exemplifying the evil in the world and pin it to a board. Pray for those involved, that they might repent and be forgiven. Then bring your own shortcomings before God.

Further stations on the Noah story might inspire prayer of different kinds by focusing on:

- the diversity of the animal kingdom, with household items of animal origin to touch or hold.
- different kinds of food, with samples to taste.
- the power of water both to destroy and to purify, with water to pour, stir or wash dirty hands.

Concluding stations might develop environmental concerns (perhaps with a campaign postcard to sign and send), or the link with baptism made explicit in 1 Peter 3:18–22 (perhaps a reading of baptismal vows and a self-signing with a cross).

While some people might prefer the simplicity of a stationless labyrinth, others will benefit more from a prayer journey with the content that stations provide. Be warned, however, that preparing one of these takes many hours, and is best done by a number of people working as a team.

Personal and corporate— reaching in and reaching out

A labyrinth with or without stations is an opportunity for an individual to be still before God and be transformed by his Spirit. The visible journey parallels an inner journey. Unlike corporate worship, the individual can choose when to tarry and savour a moment, an idea, a revelation. Yet, unlike a quiet time of prayer in your room with closed door, you may be aware of others following the same journey, so there is also a corporate dimension to this experience.

If you dare to set up a labyrinth of your own, for your church or a wider community, you will find that the planning and execution of the project are a communal exercise which draws people together. If you publicize it and make it available, even to the general public, you may be surprised by those who are drawn in to a new kind of encounter with the living God. ■

Walking the labyrinth engages the body as well as the mind

15

24–7 Prayer

Andy Freeman led the first 24–7 Boiler Room in Reading, UK. He now helps others to develop Boiler Rooms in their communities and works on 24–7's International team. He also co-authored 'Punk Monk' with Pete Grieg (Kingsway, 2007).

 It's 4.15am and I'm sitting in a room, about 20ft by 20ft. I can see bright stars in the night sky through the skylight and I know it's a cold night, having just walked in about 15 minutes before. I had regretted not putting on a coat.

I begin to scan round the room. Artwork is almost dripping from the walls and ceilings. Pictures of God, pictures to God, passionate prayers, Bible verses, questions and doubts can all be found on these scraps of paper that have formed intercessions of the marker pen or paintbrush. 'Be still and know that I am God' is written in crayon above my head. To my left, someone's written a letter to God, crying for help.

I fix my eyes on the candles in the corner of the room, the small icon of Jesus. The Sigur Ros track on the stereo drifts over me. I focus on Jesus and begin to pray, inviting him to be with me, in a little room, in the night.

Welcome to one of the many 24–7 prayer rooms which are taking place all over the world. Even as you slept last night, people were in similar rooms praying—in the UK, in Europe, in North America, in Asia and in Africa—people praying.

This has been going on for eight years now. In September 1999, the first 24–7 prayer room in Chichester sparked into life. People prayed there continuously for three months, and kick-started a movement which has now spread to 60 countries. And for many people, their story is much the same as mine—that God has changed the course of their lives through these funny, intimate and deeply holy little prayer rooms.

It was January 2000 and I was a youth worker at Greyfriars Church in Reading. Greyfriars was a growing but also reasonably typical Church of England church, on the evangelical side of things. Although church life looked OK, we were frustrated, feeling that our youth programme wasn't having much impact. So the team had all taken time off work to attend a youth leaders' conference and we were expectant that God would show us some new kind of strategy or idea. Then we read the flyer.

It read '24–7 Prayer' and had the headline 'Epidemic warning' across the bottom. It called on people to set up continuous prayer rooms and spread a virus of prayer.

'Prayer?' Was that it, God? Was that what you wanted to say to us? I have to admit I was a little disappointed to think that this was God's blinding flash of light to us. 'Here is my great strategy: you should pray more.' But as we chatted, we realized that although we had worked hard and tried lots of great ideas, we hadn't spent too much time praying. We certainly hadn't spent time praying simply

because we wanted to hang out with Jesus. 'Prayer it is, then,' we said.

Within a month we had organized a weekend of 24–7 prayer. A room was set aside and decorated. We sorted out a rota, dividing the day into hours and getting people to sign up for different slots. Then, on a Friday night at the end of February 2000, we opened.

My first slot was 3am on the Saturday. I remember going to sleep that night feeling slightly worried that

In the prayer room we began to find Jesus

I might not wake up and slightly upset that I'd have to get up in the middle of the night. But at 2.45am my alarm went off, I jumped in the car and set off.

Arriving at the door to the church centre, I was a bit concerned. It looked dark and no one was answering the bell. I took out my key, opened up and wandered down to the prayer room. I could feel my heart sinking at the thought of finding the room empty or finding someone asleep. Then Nathaniel put his head round the door, smiled and called to me to come in. 'You won't believe what's been going on...' Little did I know that that night would change the direction of my life completely.

I remember Nathaniel's grin as he explained what had been happening that first night. Our young people had been really going for it in prayer.

The walls were already covered with their heart cries, Bible verses and pictures. Everyone had remarked how easy it had been to pray.

As I prayed with Nathaniel, and with Dan who was also still there (even though his slot was due to have finished two hours previously), I began to dwell on what was going on here. I can safely say that I had never experienced God's presence so heavily. I had seen some pretty amazing stuff on my twelve-year road as a Christian. I had experienced God's meeting with me personally. I had been in meetings where God had done amazing things. But here was a space in which God's presence seemed to be residing. I didn't think my theology was meant to believe in special places or buildings. What was going on?

Our first weekend of 24–7 prayer will live long in my memory. It was followed by many other prayer rooms, and it resulted in salvation, in healings and in many answered prayers, as well as many unanswered ones. But those nights of prayer started something in our hearts, too. As we prayed together in those first weeks, people started saying, 'Why can't we have a prayer room all the time?' As people met with Jesus, there was a longing for something longer-term. The Boiler Room in Reading opened in 2001. It was a name we just made up, to be honest, expressing the idea of a place of heat or energy. We later learnt that the Baptist preacher Charles Spurgeon's mission prayer rooms were also called Boiler Rooms.

In the prayer room we began to find Jesus. We shaped rhythms of prayer that helped us to spend time with him. We lived our prayers out practically because we saw that Jesus did that, too. We valued relationship, just as Jesus did and does, and so communities developed.

Seven years on and my role in 24-7 Prayer is to help build and grow communities of prayer, mission and justice—maybe 30 of them worldwide right now—which have grown from this initial place of committing to pray. These long-term monasteries of prayer, or Boiler Rooms, are growing in the most unlikely of settings: East German villages, drug and prostitution tolerance zones in Mexico, among clubbers in Ibiza, with the Salvation Army in Liverpool.

People often ask what's going on here. For me the answer is simple. It's about Jesus, about centring on him through prayer. We have been deeply influenced by Dietrich Bonhoeffer and his dreams of new monastic communities. But much of what Bonhoeffer wrote expressed a simpler and more basic desire: 'Jesus is the only significance. Besides Jesus nothing has any significance. He alone matters' (*A Testament to Freedom*, HarperCollins, 1990).

I'm tired of strategies, of keys to growth or models of building church, because they usually don't work, and they put me and others in boxes. I'm tired most of all because they're centred on us and not on Christ.

When we began our first prayer room I didn't know much about devotion or about prayer. If I'm honest, I overworked and my spiritual life had little or no depth. There was much in terms of good intention and of passion—but it outworked itself in my strength and my activity. As 24-7's leaders met recently in Spain, we felt that God was reminding us of our call to prayer, that as a movement we should live up to our name.

Those nights of prayer
started something in our hearts

As each day goes by I become more passionate about my dream to see God move in our world and bring about change. I also become more and more convinced that this will happen through a move of prayer. ■

May I never boast except in the cross of our Lord Jesus Christ, through which the world has been crucified to me, and I to the world (Galatians 6:14, TNIV).

For more information visit www.24-7prayer.com.

Reminded of the light

Between 2001 and 2006, Brad Lincoln worked in Nepal with the International Nepal Fellowship, providing management support to the work of the mission in serving those affected by leprosy, HIV, TB, disability and poverty. He now lives with his young family in Cheshire working as a company director. BRF recently published Brad's first book 'Six Men—Encountering God'.

> Her life was almost senseless, literally without senses

Everything she once had was gone, and this shell of a woman was left where one of the nurses had thoughtfully propped her, leaning against the green cement wall in the afternoon sun to soak up a little warmth. Not that she could properly feel it, insensitive as she was to almost every stimulus. Her life was almost senseless, literally without senses, blind and robbed of taste and touch. She was oblivious even to the pressure on her bladder, and probably unaware (thank heaven for small mercies) of the sweet, stale stench of her urine-soaked clothes. Her face was expressionless as I walked towards her; the maze of wrinkles and grossly thickened skin didn't move to betray any awareness of my approach. Her watery eyes wandered aimlessly, looking slightly upwards as if seeking the answer to some recurring question. She certainly had the right to demand a few answers—'Why me?' or 'When will this all end?' Perhaps she was remembering a time before the disease.

If leprosy has a personality, it is cruel, spiteful, selfish, taking everything piece by piece and giving nothing in return, leaving nothing behind. First it takes the childhood sense of peace and invulnerability that allows the young the freedom to cavort naked in the streams and to run half bare through the green, green rice fields. As a young girl she noticed the pale patch on her arm, striking against her sun-darkened skin, and dreaded the moment when others would spot it. Each bright day would have been darkened by the fear of discovery. When the dreaded day came, she lost her name, *kanchhi*—youngest daughter—and was awarded the new epithet: *birami*—sick one, cursed one.

Those girls and boys she once skipped with were warned by their parents to stay clear from her. 'Don't touch her,' they would scold—not whispered private admonition but shouted commands within her hearing, fingers pointed, like jabbing accusations. She was banned from the village tap, getting her water from the river when no one was watching. No one would touch a plate or bowl that she had used. Even her mother was frightened, flinching when she accidentally brushed against her. For some families, similarly afflicted, the shame would be too much to bear and the leper child would be cast out to wander away from human contact in the woods, or locked in a cupboard with food occasionally pushed under a door.

In comparison the subsequent loss of her sense of hot and cold, pain and touch some years later was easier to bear, because she did not even notice its

... shame would be too much to bear and the leper child would be cast out to wander away from human contact

departure. She did not feel the blisters on her feet, even when they bled. She did not realize there was a thorn buried in her foot. Sometimes, when lifting the dented tin pots from the cooking fire, she could burn herself so badly that the skin would peel back to reveal the glistening white bone beneath. When she discovered the injuries she would hold them up to dispassionate inspection, feeling nothing more than a vague curiosity. Having lost the relationship of sensation she became emotionally detached from her own hands and feet, and they would become about as important to her as any old tatty gloves or socks, full of holes and beyond repair. She tried in vain to beg, borrow or steal the new socks she could not afford, to cover up her feet. And since she repulsed everyone she met, she certainly could not get a job or earn enough to buy gloves to cover up her threadbare hands.

Through inadvertent self-inflicted damage she lost her fingers and toes, one little cut, one infected abscess at a time. Such was the loss of sensation that she didn't even notice them go. She woke one morning with an entire finger missing, gnawed off by a rat while she slept, blessedly unaware.

Her skin lost its natural sweat response and it became parched, dry and cracked as a pre-monsoon river bed. It became taut like a drying canvas, pulling at the soles of her feet and the palms of her hand like desiccated parchment, drawing the stumps and knuckles into twisted and distorted claws. Her ankles became blackened hard and shiny, smooth to the touch as if the pores had fused together.

That wicked disease had not finished with her yet, though. The skin around her ears and lips thickened and bloated, and her nose seemed somehow to collapse back into the profile of her once fresh face. She lost control of her bladder, the use of her legs, and any independence. Dignity, pride, self-esteem had all long since gone.

Having lost the relationship of sensation she became emotionally detached

Dispassionate inspection, feeling nothing more than a vague curiosity

© Brad Lincoln

An elderly Nepali woman whose health has been affected by leprosy—though not as badly as the woman in Brad's account.

Finally, when she had fully understood how the world hated her, having seen person after person turn away in revulsion and fear, the disease shut her off. It crowded through the nerves, killing the subconscious blink response that soothes the eyes with saline balm. With supreme irony, this woman who deserved to cry so many tears lost the ability to cry, and as the surface of her eyes dried and crusted, as her pupils were scratched with dust and grime, the light faded. Slowly, gradually came the mist, then the greyness and then the failing of the light. She descended into the permanent black of blindness, a night in which there is no hope of dawn.

I had no special or professional reason to visit her. As the manager of our work in that region of Nepal, my working life comprised emails, reports, budgets, policies and meetings. In many respects it was exactly like any desk job in Swindon or Slough, Preston or Prestwick. And in common with all the other managers the world over, my bad days could be caused by nothing more than a negative message, a line of uncooperative text, or a balance sheet that wouldn't. But when the job got too much for me, when I burned with anger or frustration at lack of progress, when I despaired in the face of a funding shortage or fretted at staffing problems, I could shove

> With supreme irony, this woman who deserved to cry so many tears lost the ability to cry...

my chair back from the desk and monitor and swivel round to contemplate the soaring white Himalayas framed by my office window, the sun sparkling on their saw-tooth summits.

I am ashamed to say that on some days—normally the hottest days when the power cuts robbed us of the ceiling fans, making the still, heavy air like a hot, damp blanket—even the magnificence of God's 8000-metre monuments to his own creative power were not enough to lift my spirits or place my administrative concerns in perspective. On those days I would walk out of the admin block, perspiration rolling down my spine as I strolled through the knee-length but sparse dry grass that surrounded our hospital, heading towards the small eight-room block we called *Anand Niwas*—New Rejoicing. It was there that we housed a handful of long-term patients, all women. The cheap medication we had administered so easily had long since eradicated from their bodies the bacteria that had caused their leprosy. But we could do nothing about the deformity, the loss of sensation, and the blindness. These elderly ladies were examples of what are called in the trade 'burned out' cases. They were still with us quite simply because they had no family, nowhere else to go, no one else to care for them.

As usual, while drawing near, I tried to guess her age; probably 50 or 60, although she looked much older. I didn't know her given name. I called her *Aamaa*—mother. It was purely a recognition that she was older than me, and in Nepali society age and experience are things worthy of respect. She had no children of her own, so I hope she appreciated my giving her that honorary status.

I would approach and squat next to Aamaa. She would hear me arrive, and although she had no idea what I looked like, she would know by my accent and my schoolboy Nepali that I was the foreign missionary boss. We would talk a little, about nothing much—how she was feeling (fine), what she had eaten (rice), and other small talk.

> **We could do nothing about the deformity, the loss of sensation, and the blindness**

> I burned with anger or frustration at **lack of progress**

> As she prayed she reached out from the permanent night of her existence

And then, before I left and went back to my work, we would pray together. She would always ask if we could pray, and when we did she would always insist on praying for me.

Brought up a Hindu, dragged down to nothing by a disease, she had encountered Jesus in that missionary hospital while being treated by the Christian nurses. It was her saviour who lifted her from the depths to give her a life and, astonishingly, a gratitude for all she had received in Christ. Incredibly, she frequently thanked God for his gift of leprosy, because she felt that without it she would probably never have met him. As she prayed she reached out from the permanent night of her existence and helped me to lift my eyes from the froth of my problems to the towering substance of her faith.

I almost always went to her when burdened, and I always walked back to my office able to see once again those dazzling peaks, able to praise God, grateful for my *aamaa*. I knew and she knew that leprosy had made her the least that a human being could be. But in the spiritual dimension, of which Nepalese are naturally so much more aware than us Westerners, I believe she towers like a giant. I believe that in heaven she has escaped the darkness. She never failed to remind me that I walk in the light.

Thank you, Father. Thank you, Aamaa. ∎

If you are interested in learning more about the work of INF, visit www.inf.org.

Journeying through
darkness

Anna Brooker is Priest in Charge of All Saints Church, Isleworth in west London. Her interests include theatre, walking by the Thames, writing and learning Spanish. She is married to Nick, has three almost adult children and a youthful golden retriever.

For centuries congregations have prayed the third collect of Evening Prayer: for protection both physically and spiritually, both personally and corporately. The daily reality of darkness was and is a reminder of our need for God's light in every aspect of life. This applies to groups and communities as much as to individuals. Just as people experience highs and lows, light and darkness, so churches, too, undergo similar times. Such 'nights' are not always negative; indeed they may bring new strength and vision and be necessary to the process of church growth. No one relishes them, however, and we tend to avoid or ignore the spiritual reality of a church's experiencing 'night', rather than to

Lighten our darkness, we beseech thee, O Lord; and by thy great mercy defend us from all perils and dangers of this night... (BCP)

> The daily reality of darkness was and is a reminder of our **need for God's light**

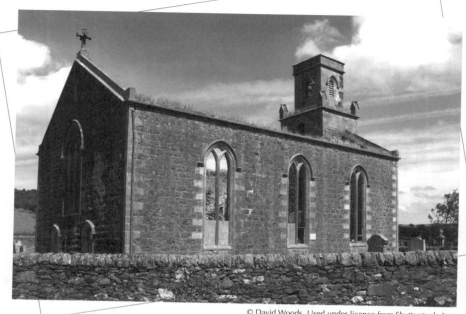

© David Woods. Used under licence from Shutterstock, Inc.

expect and prepare for such times.

Often the darkness falls when a church's leadership faces difficulties. A minister falls ill and people are shaken, anxious and fearful. In an interview some months before his death, David Watson was asked, 'Why

new strength and vision

are *you* facing terminal cancer, you who are so successful in your ministry…?' His reply was, 'Many others face it, so why *not* me?' Because society tells us we can be insured and protected against every eventuality, we are not only surprised

but also shocked and outraged when things don't go according to plan. Then when someone upon whom we depend is affected, we finally have to face the night and trust God to guide us through it.

I think of another much-loved church leader who fell ill soon after a new curate arrived. The curate contacted the church home groups and called a prayer meeting. He then led the church with great wisdom and humility for many months, upon the basis of regular, corporate prayer. By the end of his time in charge, the church was definitely stronger. Members were able to be less dependent on their clergy and had grown in practical, tangible faith. Prayer for the vicar was answered, not in miraculous or speedy ways, but in gradual and sustainable steps, and the next stages for his ministry and the church were revealed by God.

It may not be illness but relationship breakdown that plunges a church into night. The more 'high profile' the individuals concerned, the wider the impact and feelings of anger, betrayal and disillusion that result. There may even be a split in the church, causing great pain and distress. And our natural reaction is to blame, judge and criticize. The church that survives such times will do so only through the grace of God, enabling members to support, forgive and love, and to put healing of relationships as a higher priority than 'being right'. This is not to say that, at such times, there will not be divisions which become permanent, but a measure of reconciliation is still possible and necessary in order for both parties to be released from continuing and damaging effects of the split.

Sadly, night can fall gradually and seem to last interminably, when discouragement sets in and there is no sense of vision or direction for a church. A change of leadership is usually the only way out in these circumstances, and a new leader may still face months or years of darkness before dawn breaks. Often a congregation will have dwindled due to the prevailing negativity, but those who remain may be fiercely resistant to change, locked into a 'bunker' mentality. In C.S. Lewis' *The Last Battle*, we encounter a group of dwarves whose gaze is fixed to the ground where they scrabble for scraps of food, unable therefore to see the banquet laid out on the table above them, and totally unwilling to believe that it is there.

The impact of regular prayer, claiming the light of God's presence and guidance, will in time push back the darkness and attract others to the light, so that the church can begin to grow once more. It may, however, get darker before it becomes truly light. The light may be perceived as a threat

> **The impact of regular prayer,** claiming the light of God's presence and guidance, will in time push back the darkness

by some, disturbing their dimly lit comfort zone, challenging their meagre expectations, and evoking reactions that are deeply felt, aggressive or violent. This is a very hard place for a church leader or member to go. Yet even striking one match brings light into darkness and hope into despair. Striking several matches together in corporate prayer and mutual support hastens the daylight and lights the way ahead.

Night may also encroach upon a church from outside, through the opposition of individuals or groups.

... this hope and vision sustained them through the difficult decades

Two churches in our area were burned to the ground some years ago by arsonists, one of them in my parish. The corporate memory of that experience remains vivid, and local people speak of their shock and horror as they saw the flames from afar. Thankfully, the church members remained united, determined to rebuild on the site where Christians had worshipped for centuries, and this hope and vision sustained them through the difficult decades of planning, fundraising and campaigning before the new church

was built. They also learned that bricks and mortar were not the true church. We discover in and through darkness that there are many ways to relate to people and God without needing to 'see'.

The accumulation of mundane and accidental setbacks may cause a sense of nightfall on a church. Often these setbacks feature buildings, money or both. I recently went into our church to switch on temporary heating for a concert, the boiler having broken down a few days before. As I stepped in a puddle I realized that the roof was now leaking, and the stoical musicians began to practise as I mopped, aided by two volunteers. It helped us to laugh, to pray and to decide that these minor (if expensive) problems were not able to upset our faith in God, only strengthen it.

Another church faced a major financial crisis, which threatened several staff members with redundancy and an excellent community project with closure. The team meeting at which this reality was recognized and discussed was a long, heated and painful one. Thankfully it was also undergirded with prayer, and regular prayer meetings for the church were one fruit of the discussions. Another was the decision to give notice to all the affected staff: wonderfully they offered to work their notice period in the hope that finances would be found. The final strategy was to apply for funding to a number of grant-making bodies, investing staff time and energy in doing so. Four years later the project continues, having grown through numerous changes, but more firmly rooted in prayer than it was before the crisis.

As I write I am aware of several churches where the outcome of such 'dark nights' has been very different, entailing job losses and closures. It's much harder then to see the way forward and stay positive. The cycle of day and night, like the seasons of nature, can remind us that loss and change are part of life: some aspects of a church's life and ministry may be fruitful but still need to be pruned or even die to make way for what comes next.

So what can we say of the night experiences that all churches face? Firstly, while the New Testament speaks volumes about Christians being rescued from darkness and brought into God's marvellous light, it also recognizes that, in this life, we are surrounded and opposed by the powers of darkness: the great dawn of God's kingdom is not yet here.

Secondly, we should not be surprised by night. Our 'flick a switch' instant society insulates us from natural darkness. Thus a common reaction of visitors to remote areas is that they can see the night sky for the first time—the deep darkness and the

brightness of the stars within it. The people of Israel journeyed through the desert by night as well as day, following the pillar of fire at night time. Should we expect more of our journeys as churches to be undertaken at night, guided by God rather than human sight?

Finally, contemporary society encourages us to view faith in individual terms—*my* walk with God, *my* struggles, doubts, crises. Yet the

Thus night is faced with the support of others

Contemporary society encourages us to view faith in individual terms

truth that Paul expresses in 1 Corinthians 12 is that we're not meant to live separate lives as Christians, but to be mutually accountable and dependent, sharing our suffering and joys. Thus night is faced with the support of others, with the benefit of their prayer and experience, their compassion and insight. And it is faced in the certainty that the 'light shines in the darkness, and the darkness has not overcome it' (John 1:5, TNIV). ■

Crying for the Light

Veronica Zundel's 'Crying for the Light', (BRF, 2008) draws on her experiences of clinical depression over 35 years. As well as sharing her own story, she traces the particular challenges faced by Christians going through such times, including exploring relevant Bible passages. This reading reflects the deep pain of depression.

Job: why was I born?

After this Job opened his mouth and cursed the day of his birth. Job said: 'Let the day perish on which I was born, and the night that said, "A man-child is conceived." Let that day be darkness! May God above not seek it, or light shine on it. Let gloom and deep darkness claim it. Let clouds settle upon it; let the blackness of the day terrify it. That night—let thick darkness seize it! let it not rejoice among the days of the year; let it not come into the number of the months. Yes, let that night be barren; let no joyful cry be heard in it... Let the stars of its dawn be dark; let it hope for light, but have none; may it not see the eyelids of the morning—because it did not shut the doors of my mother's womb, and hide trouble from my eyes.'

JOB 3:1–7, 9–10 (NRSV)

One thing I've noticed among depressed people is that birthdays, which should be a reason for celebration, are often positively disliked. Perhaps it's because birthdays bring us together with family members whose company we may not enjoy, or because they remind us that we are getting older and haven't achieved what we think we 'should' have done by that age.

I don't know if birthdays were celebrated in Old Testament times, but Job, suffering multiple bereavements, having lost almost everything and everyone that mattered to him, sees the day he was born as a day that should never have happened. To wish we had never been born is perhaps the worst feeling we can have. Only the truly desperate think in this way.

The trouble is, when we are really low, all we can remember are the disappointments, hurts and mistakes of our life. The good memories might as well not exist, because we can't believe in them any more and they don't seem enough to balance out the bad. Our whole life feels like a mistake.

Easy answers such as 'God doesn't make junk' are no real help because they don't reach down into the deep sadness and self-hatred. The best we can do at such moments is to hang on to the knowledge that these times pass—because they do. ■

When we are really low, all we can remember are the disappointments

Prayer

'You knit me together in my mother's womb' (Psalm 139:13). God, help me to believe it.

I bring this candle,
I acknowledge the
darkness...

Music for the soul:

St John's Night on a Bare Mountain

Gordon Giles is vicar of St Mary Magdalene's Church, Enfield, north London. He contributes to BRF's 'New Daylight' notes and has also written 'The Music of Praise' (2002), 'The Harmony of Heaven' (2003), 'O Come, Emmanuel' (2005) and 'Fasting and Feasting' (2008) for BRF.

For once you were darkness, but now in the Lord you are light. Live as children of light—for the fruit of the light is found in all that is good and right and true.

EPHESIANS 5:8–9 (NRSV)

Spirituality, like many aspects of our life, has a darker side. The *Star Wars* films are upfront about this when they refer to the 'the dark side', and the Austrian psychoanalyst Sigmund Freud described the mind as having a brightly lit West End and a dark and dingy East End, drawing on a common perception of Victorian London geography. St John of the Cross wrote of 'the dark night of the soul', describing spiritual dryness and the awareness of the absence of God, and there is a sense in which our inner life can enter a period of 'night' if and when we experience spiritual bleakness, pain or doubt.

There is another form of spiritual darkness which is far more sinister and has little, if any, light in the distance: the dark spirituality of witchcraft, sorcery and necromancy. These three are flatly condemned in the Bible, but are still prevalent even in our enlightened, science-obsessed world. Leviticus 19:26 forbids witchcraft, and the magician Simon is condemned for confusing the apostles' miracles with sorcery in Acts 8:9–24. King Saul seeks out a medium at Endor in 1 Samuel 28:7, and since Leviticus 20:27 declares necromancy (communicating with the dead) to be a capital offence, it comes as no surprise to find in 1 Chronicles 10:13 that Saul's consulting a medium is given as a contributing factor in his demise. There can be no doubt that no Christian should have anything to do with such practices, which involve forces of evil that are real and dangerous.

Yet these phenomena hold a strange attraction, not least in art and literature. Ghost and horror stories abound, and some have inspired composers to portray in music the scenes that surround a 'Witches' Sabbath'. The French composer Hector Berlioz (1803–69) set the final movement of his *Symphonie Fantastique* at a Witches' Sabbath, and in 1867 Modest Mussorgsky wrote his infamous 'St John's Night on a Bare Mountain'. The St John in the title is not John of the Cross, nor is this the dark night of the soul; Mussorgsky's nocturne is set on 23 June, the eve of the feast day of the birth of John the Baptist. We might not associate John with death, but within the Russian Orthodox

tradition he is said to have descended into the realm of the dead and preached the advent of Christ. John is also said to appear to those who have not heard the gospel of Christ just before they die, giving them a final opportunity to be saved. Consequently Orthodox churches often display an icon of John prominently and Tuesdays are dedicated to his memory. Thus we can understand how the night before his festival becomes a night of necromancy and witchcraft (as Halloween, the night before All Saints' Day, has become in Western tradition).

> ... dark as Mussorgsky's night is, it is ended by the ringing of a church bell heralding the **light of dawn**

Mussorgsky (1839–81) was not a particularly pleasant character and had a tendency to drunkenness. It may well have been after a drunken evening with a copy of Nikolai Gogol's book of short stories *Evenings on a Farm Near Dikanka* on his lap that Mussorgsky wrote his strange and sinister piece. 'St John's Eve', written in 1831, is the second story in Gogol's collection and tells of two lovers, Petro and Pidorka, who are parted by Pidorka's father. Petro then meets Basavriuk, who is said to be

No matter how deep the night, there is always the light of Christ bringing healing and release from sin

The night is not necessarily a place for fear or evil

the devil. He leads him to gold, but Petro can only claim it by finding a fern that blooms on St John's Eve, and by killing, which he does. The lovers marry, but Pidorka consults a witch; the child Petro murdered to get the treasure returns to haunt him, and Petro is carried off by the devil. Pidorka eventually goes on a pilgrimage, but everyone leaves the village because the devil and the evil spirits cannot be exorcized.

We cannot simply say that this is the story behind 'Night on a Bare Mountain', as Mussorgsky's music went through many revisions and had other inspirations, too. He set out a four-part programme: '1: An underground noise of inhuman voices. Appearance of the Spirits of Darkness followed by an appearance of Satan. 2: His adoration. 3: A Black Mass. 4: Joyful dancing of the Witches' Sabbath. All of which is ended by the ringing of a church bell and the appearance of dawn.' There are various versions of the piece, including a choral setting and a version in Act 3 of the opera *Sorochintsy Fair* (1873). Mussorgsky's rather more sober and devout colleague Nikolai Rimsky-Korsakov (1844–1908) rewrote and arranged the piece, omitting parts that were religiously offensive, such as the parody of an Orthodox chant in the section that describes a Black Mass during which Satan is worshipped. The version that we most often hear today is Rimsky-Korsakov's, or perhaps the arrangement that made the piece world-famous: that by Leopold Stokowski used in Disney's *Fantasia*.

Given its pedigree, why should we take an interest in Mussorgsky's nightmarish music? Firstly, it is important that we understand what this piece is all about, because it is so popular and widely heard. Most people who hear it on the radio or watch *Fantasia* with their children have no idea what the composer had in mind. Secondly, we can notice that dark as Mussorgsky's night is, it is ended by the ringing of a church bell heralding the light of dawn. For no matter how deep the night or wicked the world, there is always the light of Christ bringing healing and release from sin. We might recall the words of Paul: 'The night is far gone, the day is near. Let us then lay aside the works of darkness and put on the armour of light' (Romans 13:12). And we can also remember that the night is not necessarily a place for fear or evil, that the Lord is with us even when we enter dark places or lie down at night to sleep: 'By day the Lord commands his steadfast love, and at night his song is with me, a prayer to the God of my life' (Psalm 42:8). Mussorgsky's dramatic but devilish tone poem is not a danger to us if we wear the armour of light and sing the Lord's song, even in the very depth of night. ∎

Readings for reflection

Ephesians 5:6–17

Music to listen to

St John's Night on a Bare Mountain by Mussorgsky. There are many recordings, including a budget one, (ref: Naxos 8.557645), which is the arrangement by Stokowski used in *Fantasia*. The Bournemouth Symphony Orchestra is directed by Jose Serebrier, 1997.

PRAYER

Lord of light and night, you protect us in day and darkness. Keep us faithful to our calling as children of light, and drive away from us wickedness and fear, that we may always be drawn to worship you alone. Amen

Vigil

Lessons for the night

Emma Garrow works as a freelance writer. She is a member of the South West Spiritual Directors' Network and volunteers with a hospital chaplaincy visiting team.

It is Saturday night and the Christians in Troas are gathering to break bread. Paul is with them, on the eve of his departure. They stay until midnight, listening to his preaching. Then terror strikes. One of their number, Eutychus, is overcome by drowsiness, falls from the window ledge where he has been sitting and is killed. Paul takes Eutychus in his arms and revives him before the company. Bread is broken once more and the meeting continues until dawn, when Paul departs.

Some scholars believe this account from Acts 20 to be the first record of a church gathering in vigil. It is a practice exemplified by Jesus himself in the garden of Gethsemane.

The word we use is from the Latin for 'wakefulness', *vigilia*. If we read the news headlines, we find that it crops up time and again as a cause or campaign holds a vigil in support of the troubled, to make known the plight of the poor or disadvantaged. In private life we may hold vigil at the bedside of a sick or dying loved one.

For the Church a vigil has always been something equally deliberate, an act of devotion, of worship, most often associated with the eve of the principal feasts in the Church's year. Though not every vigil is characterized by such trauma as befell the church at Troas during Paul's visit, it is a practice concerned with watching, waiting and overcoming.

On those nights when wakefulness overtakes us and our thoughts dwell on what concerns us most, we may find ourselves turning to prayer as we mull over hopes and fears. Could our night-time musings, although not liturgical, not planned, become a vigil as we watch and wait for sleep to carry us to dawn? It is not just at Christmas, at Easter or at any of the other festivals that we can draw on the message of God's power to overcome darkness. Each vigil night in the Church's year can remind us of how we can bring the night-time workings of our mind into the light of God's presence.

Christmas

The vigil that is Midnight Mass is perhaps the most accessible and atmospheric of all the Church's night watches for a major celebration. The thought of it evokes an instantly familiar range of sensations to do with candles, carols and coming home to mince pies. It is the vigil that those not used to going to church may make a special attempt to attend. And this is highly appropriate, because at the Christmas Eve vigil we watch and wait

with a sure and certain hope for the morning when we will celebrate the Incarnation, the moment when God became man, making himself accessible to everyone.

We think of Christmas as a special time of year, unique in its smells, flavours and atmosphere. At Midnight Mass we look for an event that promises the presence of God. This means that on ordinary nights, when in the darkness no candles are lit, we can know that the Christ who came then is with us now.

... a practice concerned with **watching, waiting and overcoming**

Epiphany

We may think of Epiphany as the day for taking down the Christmas decorations, yet its true meaning is a further celebration of the 'manifestation' of Christ to the world. The Eastern Church focuses on Christ's baptism, while in the West we remember the visit of the magi to Bethlehem. In the Church of England, the season of Epiphany begins with Evening Prayer on Epiphany Eve, that is, Twelfth Night.

The visit of the magi reveals more about the gift of Christ—he is to be the revelation of God to the whole world, not just to his own people. It is a festival that celebrates reconciliation, the coming together of God and humankind, and the unity that can now be possible between peoples.

As we take down our Christmas cards, perhaps we sneak another look at the messages and recall the friends who remembered us this year. Perhaps we can add their names to our prayers when sleep eludes and we lie awake at night.

⌐ ... an openness to the Spirit that can lead to a kindling of our own creativity

Easter is the ultimate celebration of overcoming

Candlemas

Candlemas marks the day when Jesus was presented in the temple (Luke 2:22–40). It comes 40 days after Christmas, since it was 40 days after his birth that Jesus was ritually dedicated to God according to Jewish law. It is also the time when Mary attained purification following childbirth.

Luke narrates that at the temple the holy family met Simeon, whose prayer on seeing Jesus the newborn is used as the *Nunc Dimittis* in Evening Prayer: 'Now, Lord, you let your servant go in peace'.

The singer Patti Boulaye recalled in an interview once how her mother had taught her, 'If you can't sleep, ask the Lord what he is trying to say to you.' Sometimes it is something we have missed, or something we have done, that keeps us from rest.

Patti's prayer reminds us to check with God. Simeon's prayer reminds us that when God has helped us to deal with whatever may be preventing our sleep, we truly can return to peace.

Annunciation

Nine months before Christmas, the Church marks the moment when the angel Gabriel announced to Mary that she would bear the Christ. It is from the Annunciation that we have the *Magnificat*, Mary's response to her good news (Luke 1:46–55) and a familiar prayer in liturgical worship.

Mary's vision came to her all of a sudden, unexpectedly. Those hours in the night when we fail to sleep are not necessarily troubling. Sudden insights and understandings dawn; we glimpse a new light and discover an openness to the Spirit that can lead to a kindling of our own creativity.

Easter

Easter is the ultimate celebration of overcoming. Christ has passed through death and returned to life, enabling all to partake in life's feast for ever. The Church lights the paschal candle on Holy Saturday night and rises early on Easter morning to watch for the sunrise. Then the shout goes up: 'Christ is risen! Alleluia!'

Before Easter there has been Gethsemane and the cross. Should life be tough and our nights filled with a troubled wakefulness, there is one thing we can know: dawn will break. Though our troubles may not evaporate with the darkness, because of the resurrection we can also know that 'When I awake, I am still with you' (Psalm 139:18, NIV).

Pentecost

Pentecost is about both gift and calling. Jesus told his disciples to wait for the promised gift of the Holy Spirit. When this gift was poured out, dramatic results ensued. The company of previously frightened disciples grew into a strong and burgeoning community, which over time became the worldwide Church. Occurring on the seventh Sunday after Easter, Pentecost marks this moment in history with a renewed vision to fulfil the Church's mission.

Sometimes it is weariness with our role in life that causes lack of sleep. Stress, duty or lack of purpose keep us from rest in the night and from vigour during the day. What we need is the touch of God's Spirit reminding us who we are and what he is calling us to be in his name.

All Saints' Day

The eve of All Saints' Day is Halloween, now known as a festival of horrors and ghouls that many Christians try to avoid or to counteract with 'a party of light'. All Saints' Day commemorates those whose dedication to Christ led to their canonization, in some cases as a result of martyrdom. These saints of the past did not seek out evil but did not run from it either. They faced it out, secure in the knowledge of eternal life.

All Saints' Day also honours every saint, even those whose lives have gone unrecorded. When troubles outside our control rob us of rest and haunt us in the dead of night, making us feel afraid and alone, we can remember the lives of all those we knew personally or have heard of, who overcame fear with trust in the God of life.

There is one thing we can know: dawn will break

The Church has used vigil as part of its commemoration and worship since its foundation. Watching attentively on the eve of its principal feasts for mornings of hopefulness, the people of God are revived again for the everyday and prepared for the coming dawn.

On our ordinary nights we want to sleep, to rest, to ready ourselves for the morning. But when this need remains unfulfilled, recalling the special qualities of one of the feast vigils could help us to prepare for another day, making ourselves ready for some fresh touch of God on our lives. ■

Wilderness
sojourn

Cindy Crosby is the author of four books, including 'By Willoway Brook: Exploring the Landscape of Prayer' (Paraclete Press, 2004). Her writing appears in such publications as 'Books & Culture', 'Publishers Weekly', 'Mars Hill Review' and 'Backpacker' magazine. She and her husband, Jeff, live in the Chicago suburbs.

What eludes me in the day becomes clearer at night...

The tremolo of a loon calls me from a deep sleep. Despite the warm cocoon around me I sense the chilly air and come awake in a rush of consciousness. I'm in my sleeping bag, alone in the dark on a remote island off the coast of Canada. Night comes slowly here, and the blackness tells me it is well after midnight.

Again the loon calls, urgently. A message for me? 'Come out, come out. Come see.' Sock footed, I slide out of my sleeping bag and unzip the tent fly. Lake Superior spreads out before me, lapping at the black basalt rock that makes a sandless beach along the shore. The balsam- and spruce-scented June air smells like Christmas. Inhaling deeply, wrapped again in my sleeping bag, I settle on to the rocks.

Orion strides across the sky, chasing the moon, with Mars close on his heels, all fire and ice. The universe shimmers with sequins. Day, with its kaleidoscope colours, is gone, leaving the stirred embers of its palette: blacks and golds, silvers and sapphires.

Night, night, so bright. The universe kindles mysteries. I trace the handle of the Plough with my eyes, then follow its angle to the North Star, an unchanging compass in a changeable world. The water throws back sparks of starlight. Cold and dark, wide and deep, the lake cradles the galaxies.

When I was a child, I'd wait for twilight, then scramble up to the roof of the house. Flat on my back on the tarry shingles, I'd soak up constellations, a symphony of silence in the chambers of the night. Vast. So unknown. As the oldest sibling and the first grandchild on both sides of the family, I believed I was the axis around which the universe revolved. The night sky whispered to me differently. Hours spent on the roof spoke of the enormity of time and space, and my own small place in it.

The night sky wheels its patterns and pictures. The lake below replies with its rhythmic dance. I wonder who I am, caught between both.

A friend brought me some crocus bulbs one winter, too late to put into the frozen ground. The instructions said if I wanted the bulbs to bloom, I should keep them in a cool dark place for several months. They needed the cold and the night to grow.

Night. In my waking hours, a confusion of sounds and sights clamour for my attention. At night, I am a focused, interior creature. What eludes me in the day becomes clearer at night. I pause and rest, then open and bloom.

Something shuffles through the underbrush behind me. There's a scrabbling in the twigs, then an uneasy silence. My eyes search the woods, but I see nothing in the blackness. The loon on the lake falls silent.

Wolves on the island hunt at night, looking for young moose calves easily separated from their mothers. The howls of the pack resemble notes of a primordial flute. When I hear them from the shelter of

The wolf that does hunt me is fear

my sleeping bag, the sound jolts me instantly awake, a response written in my genes from ancient times. This primeval fear sets my heart racing, although I know with my head that the wolves aren't hunting me. The wolf that does hunt me is fear. It finds me more often than I'd like.

I am most alive, most awake in the middle of the night. But I'm afraid of the dark, prone to nightmares. I'm scared of the noises in the brush behind me and the loneliness of the vast vault of the universe over my head. Twin to my fear is a desire for something that can come only in moments when I live in that fear and drink in great gulps of starlight.

Much of my life is spent keeping the fear-wolves at bay. I use many tactics: white noise, busyness, too much talking, even reading, which is my primary tactic to shut out any unpleasantness and retreat into a world of my own. In the shadows of wilderness, I am willing to meet the wolves of fear. I let my mind run down trails I ignore in the day.

Night is when I open the door to the ghosts of memory. Disappointments and deaths. Worry and dread. Words said and words left unsaid. Fears and failures. One by one, they become visible in the dark,

like a photo negative in a developing tray. But my fear becomes less when I face it.

I come to terms with as much as I can, then practise making peace with my past and letting go of controlling my future. I release my fear into the night and the hands of the one who made it.

The night exhales in a cool breath of air. The Milky Way galaxy throws its enormous net of stars across the black sea of the universe. Mars glistens, gold and blue, gold and blue. I could touch it if I tried.

Again, the loon calls from across the lake. This time, another one answers. Waves murmur against the rocks, an eternal liquid conversation. I know that the stars I see above me may no longer be there. The radiance from extinguished stars continues to travel long after the star is gone, sometimes for millions of years. But their light is no less bright.

The bitterness of the night penetrates my sleeping bag, and I'm numb to the bone. Stiffly, I stand and look once more over the lake and sky, glittering with diamonds. The waves softly lick the rocks.

I think of Victor Hugo, who wrote: 'Go to sleep in peace. God is awake.' I slip back into my tent and wait for the dawn. ■

Night is when I open the door to the ghosts of memory. **Worry and dread**

Winter evening

At four o'clock
the winter sun
dodges the sullen mattress of the overcast
blazes an instant glory
and subsides
to smudge the west with rust.

Where are the plans
that made this morning special?
the hopes that made
the getting out of bed worthwhile?
Altered by circumstance
and winter lethargy,
trimmed by the humdrum,
but partly realized (if that),
half done,
at best.

Now understand,
this evening,
life is,
and always was,
each hazy and uncertain day,
a trusting,
hand-in-hand with God,
a step-by-step affair.

And anyway,
The sun will rise tomorrow.

FRANCIS BUXTON

Burrswood

A Christian hospital and place of healing

Dr Gareth Tuckwell moved to Burrswood Hospital as Chief Executive in September 2007, having been Clinical Director at

Hospice in the Weald. He is a trustee of Macmillan Cancer Support, chair of trustees of 'hospice23' (a Christian charity providing education and support to those working in palliative care) and an elder of Tunbridge Wells Christian Fellowship.

'For Christ's love compels us…'

2 CORINTHIANS 5:14 (NIV).

L At the heart of the 220-acre Burrswood estate that is tucked away in the glorious Kent countryside near Tunbridge Wells is a unique 33-room hospital, registered with the Healthcare Commission as an independent non-surgical provider that combines the Christian healing ministry with orthodox medical treatment and care.

How did such a place come about? On 18 February 1912, Dorothy Kerin, a young woman of 22, lay dying of tubercular meningitis. The doctors said she was unlikely to survive the night and her

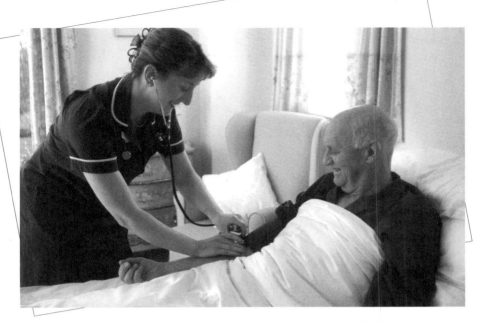

family was gathered around her bed. She suddenly sat up and said, 'Do you not hear? I am well. I must get up and walk.' Get up she did, there and then. When the doctor came the next morning he found his patient fully restored to health, with flesh on her previously emaciated body. Tests revealed no trace of her tuberculosis. She was miraculously cured.

Dorothy described in her book *The Living Touch* (Bell, 1917) how, during the fortnight prior to her healing, when she had been in a coma, she had received a vision of the Lord asking her, 'Will you go back?' She said she was charged 'to heal the sick, comfort the sorrowing and give faith to the faithless'. In 1930 a gift from a friend enabled her to renovate a house to begin her ministry to those who were sick and hurting. Her

work expanded until she owned seven properties in the street.

In 1948 she moved to Burrswood, which began as a registered nursing home where orthodox medical care was combined with Christian prayer and counsel to create a place of healing for the whole person: body, mind and spirit. Dorothy Kerin died in 1963 and since then her work has been taken forward by a Trust that bears her name.

Today Burrswood pioneers treatment, care and ministry based on a profound understanding of the relationship between conventional medicine and Christian healing. This special care is central to the Burrswood philosophy with its commitment to being a place of healing and hope for body, mind and spirit. Treatment is focused on

individual needs. It is carried out in a nurturing environment of safety and love where medical and nursing care are fully integrated with counselling, physiotherapy and Christian ministry. Burrswood today specializes in the unique needs associated with:

- post-surgical and medical care
- rehabilitation and physical therapy
- counselling, psychological and behavioural issues
- chronic fatigue syndrome
- short-term respite care
- palliative and terminal care

There are 330 people involved with the work—full timers, part timers and voluntary staff.

Those who come as patients find that their inner journey can be shared in the confidence that the depth of their need will be heard and understood. Those who are caring find that they have, above all, to listen to God, seeking the mind of Christ for the one who is sick as they try to hold their pastoral hearts and professional minds alongside the certainty that Jesus longs to bring healing and wholeness.

We see technology as the servant of humankind, not its master. We pray over the pills, encourage the patient to have a say in their treatment as much as is practicable and try to ensure that our nursing authority lies in authenticity—a modelling of how to be, as well as how to do. Often our hands are empty: we share our humanity and the seeming helplessness of some who are staying with us in the hospital.

The team have to wrestle daily with the question of whether to pray for miraculous physical healing despite the medical circumstances, or to accept that that is just the desire of their own hearts. We reflect that perhaps God is less interested in whether one of our legs is longer than the other than he is concerned to heal those who cannot love themselves, let alone their neighbour. Miraculous healing and ongoing suffering are realities of today. In this paradox we have to seek the mind of Christ, knowing that within the purposes of our sovereign God, who one day will make all things new, is a beautiful harmony between the power of prayer and our God-given offering of medicine that opens the way to wholeness.

The care of the dying is part of our ministry. The love and security of the caring community brings about a situation in which emotional, psychological and spiritual distress sometimes cease to be masked, once physical pain is eased by the medical team. We have to accept that some may choose to retain the latter to stop other forms of distress from surfacing: clinging to known pain may feel preferable to allowing an inner world to be exposed.

The late Henri Nouwen wrote, 'Compassion asks us to go where it hurts, to share in problems, fear, and anguish. Compassion challenges us

Miraculous healing and ongoing suffering are realities of today

to cry out with those in misery, to mourn with those who are lonely, to weep with those in tears. Compassion requires us to be weak with the weak, vulnerable with the vulnerable and powerless with the powerless. Compassion means full immersion in the condition of being human' (*Compassion*, DLT, 1982). In other words, compassion means being like Jesus. And that is our challenge!

Burrswood's church of Christ the Healer is central to the whole-person ministry of healing, and the chaplains are integral within the interdisciplinary team. Healing services with the laying on of hands are held twice a week alongside traditional and sacramental ministry and informal prayer. The hospital and guest house at Burrswood are adjacent to the church. The proclamation of the gospel brings healing today, enabling people to hear and enter into the living truth of the risen Christ and his salvation; the imparting of love and acceptance bring blessing and healing.

Last year thousands received the ministry of the laying on of hands at Burrswood—all individual sacramental acts, personal and special, each one an act of grace to the glory of God.

God honours this active prayer

... a total acceptance of that person, however wretched and untouchable they feel

The laying on of hands is an act of identifying with one another, of accepting that person in their need. The 'touch of Christ' is made with prayer and compassion, offering a total acceptance of that person, however wretched and untouchable they feel. This acceptance is not only in Christ but also as part of the body of Christ. It is as if the hands of the whole community are with the minister's hands offering up their love and prayer for the one in need. There are no passing spectators in the body of Christ.

Some come to receive the laying on of hands for another, perhaps because there is no such ministry in their own church. God honours this 'active prayer' where someone has the role of bridging the distance between Christ and the sufferer. In administering the laying on of hands we are alongside those for whom we pray, sharing in their pain and distress and in lifting all to God.

Anointing and the Eucharist are important areas of ministry. Confession can also be an important step towards healing. Indeed the church of Christ the Healer has been described as the outpatient department at Burrswood, although in reality that lies close by in a wing built just a decade ago. Sin, inadequacy and confusion can be acknowledged in a time of generous frankness rather than scrupulous self-concern. Then there is a sharing in that prayer of self-surrender to the Father which Jesus accomplished on the cross, in the grace of the Holy Spirit. There comes a deeper relationship with God and a sharing in his joy.

If Burrswood is to be a sign of the kingdom, it must reveal a new kind of humanity. It is not just a collection of people with personal faith who have been called to be alongside the sick and wounded, for it is the relatedness of these individuals that is the key to living out the gospel. Those 'in Christ' must allow nothing to stand in the way of unity: that includes convictions, no matter how passionately they are held. It also includes practices, attitudes, assumptions and fears. We are members in Christ, one of another, no matter how diverse we are: this even means joyfully accepting the differences in theological expression among us. There is strength in unity that springs from diversity.

We believe the ministry of healing should not be focused on the performing of miracles but rather on seeing the healing power and presence of Jesus who transforms lives. This transformation may be manifested physically, emotionally, spiritually or in relationships. Those who receive will recognize God's power at work. They will experience the care of a loving Father and be healed in ways they did not expect, with the fruit of evangelism being found at the heart of healing. Occasionally something happens that makes our spirits soar like eagles; now and then someone will get up and run, but more often we see people becoming whole, able to carry on more fully in their everyday lives. Our lives are lived in the day-to-day responsibilities and practicalities of our work, in the ordinariness of life—and that is surely where we are needed most!

As Burrswood celebrates its 60th year it faces one of its greatest challenges in monetary terms. The community is extending the hospital and carrying out a major

⌐ ... the healing power and presence of Jesus ⌐

refurbishment of the original house. It's a gracious, Grade II listed building, but tired. Work began this year, the diamond anniversary of Dorothy Kerin's arrival at Burrswood. Although the upgrading work is essential for running and cost efficiency, the key motivation is the benefit to our patients.

We currently run a bursary scheme which subsidizes patients of limited financial means. Our goal is to treble our ability to admit patients regardless of their ability to pay, thus allowing us to improve and extend patient care. £2,650,000 is the target for our hospital appeal. We have so far secured almost £1.2m and we are praying that 1500 people who believe in this ministry will be called to raise or give £1000 to enable us to go 'forward in care'. We would greatly value your prayers, too. ■

For more information about Burrswood Hospital, visit **www.burrswood.org.uk.**

An endearing saint
Nicholas

Jean Watson, an ex-MK (missionary kid) brought up in China, trained as a teacher but took up writing when her three children were small and is now a grandmother to their five children. She has completed her training as a spiritual director.

Christians are addressed as saints

'Why, who makes much of a miracle?' So wrote Walt Whitman (1819–92). And I want to say: Why, who makes much of a saint? Who, what are they? Someone devoted to God or to other people, or both? Does a saint have to be a public figure with some outstanding claim to fame such as, perhaps, miraculous powers? Or can he or she be an 'ordinary' Christian, since Christians are addressed as saints in several places in the New Testament? And in any case, aren't we all—official or unofficial saints— flawed human beings and hence merely saints in the making during our time on earth?

My mind buzzing along these lines, I began to research the life of Nicholas—officially designated as a saint within Catholic and Orthodox traditions and honoured within Protestantism.

What emerged from the records was a man devoted both to God and to people, single-mindedly and passionately so; also someone who held public office within the Christian Church for many years, becoming well known during his lifetime and even more famous afterwards as truth and legend became interwoven in his story. He was said to have performed a number of miracles, including the raising of the dead. What isn't, I think, in doubt, is that he was born in about AD270 in Patara, an area of modern Turkey then influenced by Greek culture but under Roman rule.

His fairly wealthy Christian parents died when Nicholas was still a young man. He is said, then, to have obeyed Christ's words to the rich young ruler (see Matthew 19:16–22) by giving away his money and possessions and becoming a priest. Along with other Christians at the time, he endured persecution when Diocletian was Emperor but he survived that and, unusually for a 'saint' in that era, died peacefully in his early 70s.

As a young man, he was made Bishop of Myra and gained a reputation for his good deeds, particularly for his generosity towards the poor and the vulnerable such as children and people falsely accused. There is a story about a poor man who had three daughters for whom he could not afford the dowries that would ensure good marriages for them. Learning of this, Nicholas went secretly to the poor man's house and threw in three bags of gold to ensure that the girls would marry good husbands. According to one account he threw one bag down the chimney; in another version, the bag or bags landed in a shoe—hence, perhaps, St Nicholas, along with Santa Claus, coming to be associated with entry to homes via chimneys, and gifts placed in shoes or stockings.

There are also several stories about Nicholas's intervening successfully on behalf of people whom he believed to have been unjustly accused or jailed. And in an account of his pilgrimage to the Holy Land, he is said to have saved the life of a sailor who fell overboard during a storm that was buffeting the boat in which they were travelling.

From all this, it's not hard to see why Nicholas came to be celebrated as the gift-giver and as the patron saint of sailors, children and the poor, the powerless and disadvantaged. Many churches all over Europe were named after him and his feast day is now celebrated in many places all over the world, in different ways and on different dates.

Over time, the names Santa Claus, derived from the Dutch *Sinterklaas*, and Father Christmas came to be associated

Nicholas came to be celebrated as the gift-giver

with him, but in some countries the life and legacy of St Nicholas are still celebrated in their own right—and perhaps that's how it should be. Certainly the modern Father Christmas/Santa Claus overtones can make for the devaluation and commercialization of the true meaning and message of Christmas: the birth of the Christ-child.

Often goodness is portrayed as **passive and spineless**

Back to my original questions. I have to admit, I am personally rather uncomfortable with canonizing people, or indeed putting people on any sort of pedestal. But this is not to suggest that we shouldn't appreciate and be inspired by and grateful for the commendable lives and qualities of other Christians down the centuries as well as of those living today. Henry Wadsworth Longfellow's (1807–82) take on this thought is expressed more memorably (from 'Psalms of Life'):

Lives of great men all remind us,
We can make our lives sublime,
And, departing, leave behind us
Footsteps on the sands of time.

I also like George Eliot's (1819–80) depiction in *Middlemarch* of a very much less public saint, who happens to be a woman. Of this person, Dorothea, she wrote in *Middlemarch*: 'Her full nature spent itself in deeds which left no great name on the earth but the effect of her being on those around her was incalculable, for the growing good of the world is partly dependent on unhistoric acts and on all those Dorotheas who live faithfully their hidden lives and rest in unvisited graves.'

It's equally important, I believe, to celebrate goodness, whether it is evidenced in the lives of 'great' (in other words, famous) people or in those who quietly live out the lines written by John Wesley (1703–91):

Do all the good you can,
By all the means you can,
In all the ways you can,
In all the places you can,
At all the times you can,
To all the people you can,
As long as ever you can.

One small but vital PS: so often goodness is portrayed as passive and spineless; the 'bad' characters in novels are often more engaging and exciting than the 'good' ones. But genuine goodness, genuine saintliness, can't be like that, can it? 'A saint is one who makes goodness attractive,' wrote Laurence Housman (1865–1959). And I think the accounts that we have of St Nicholas show that, at the very least, he qualified for that definition. ∎

Bringing hope

in the night

Sister Ann M. Baldwin CSC is a retired psychotherapist who is now engaged in practising creative writing. She has been a member of the Community of the Sisters of the Church for around 50 years, having previously served in the Women's Auxiliary Air Force (WAAF) during World War II.

The Community of the Sisters of the Church was founded in 1870, the result of the vision of a remarkable woman, Emily Ayckbowm. Born the daughter of an Anglican clergyman in 1836, her life spanned most of the Victorian era. The poverty and social deprivation of the poor who lived in slums forming part of her father's parish in Chester stirred Emily's deeply religious conscience and she sought ways to alleviate their distress.

A brief visit to London made Emily realize that her work for the poor would have a wider influence were it to be centred in the capital. When opportunity arose she sold her Chester home and took up residence in a poverty-stricken area of north-west London. It was from there that the Community of the Sisters of the Church was founded, with the

Children of the poor
were uneducated and she built schools...

encouragement of the vicar of the new St Augustine's Church, Kilburn.

Here Emily saw the poor in even worse circumstances than those she had seen in Chester and she set about practical means to address their needs. She saw the hungry and provided soup kitchens offering inexpensive meals; she saw the ill-clad and provided depots where second-hand inexpensive clothing could be bought. She saw that children of the poor were uneducated and she built schools;

55

The Sisters and children were scattered to places of safety

seeing that they lacked care after illness, she built convalescent homes as a respite from airless and unhealthy housing. There were orphans and foundlings and she founded orphanages, as they were then called. Later the Sisters renamed them 'children's homes'.

The Kilburn convent that Emily built remained the Mother House of the Community until the Second World War, when a bomb devastated the building. The Sisters and children under their care were scattered to places of safety, where they remained until the war was over. In 1949 the Sisters, unable to return to their London convent, found a new home and settled in a totally different area.

St Michael's Convent in Richmond, Surrey, was indeed a far cry from the original setting of Emily Ayckbowm's choice for her work in the 19th century, but it proved a fitting place for the Sisters' work as they recognized the needs of the 20th century.

By the 1970s the Sisters had transferred all their large institutions, such as schools and homes, either to the Church or to government agencies, where social conscience was beginning to bite. Other works begun by Emily Ayckbowm had become obsolete as they were taken over by a Welfare State.

There are always some unfortunate ones who fall outside the net of the Welfare State, however. The Sisters are now trying to meet their need from a community house in the red light district of inner-city Bristol, where their work is, in fact, a natural successor to Emily's mission to the poor of the 19th century.

From the Bristol house, Sisters reach out to prostitutes who work the streets by night and to men who, for one reason or another, are jobless and needy, ready to turn to crime, or have served prison sentences and been released only to return to a bleak existence. From this unlikely source a sizeable company of women and men aid the Sisters in dispensing food parcels and undertaking practical jobs about the house. They befriend the needy as they have, in their turn, been befriended.

Apart from the work in Bristol, the Community now turns its attention to other needs that characterize the 21st century: people who have lost their Christian roots in an increasingly secular Western culture.

It seems paradoxical that, while in the Victorian era it was material deprivation that had to be tackled before spiritual needs could be addressed, now it is material plenty which often stands in the way of addressing spiritual poverty.

Victor Frankl, a Jewish psychiatrist who spent some years in a Nazi concentration camp, observed that 'man cannot live on welfare alone'! Earlier Carl Jung, the Swiss psychiatrist, said much the same thing: 'About a third of my cases are not suffering from a clinically definable neurosis but from the senselessness of their lives.'

Emily Ayckbowm told her Sisters that the work they undertook must necessarily be adapted to meet the changing conditions of a particular age. Today's Sisters of the Church have adapted their educational role to a secular society which has lost its roots in Christianity and seeks to fill that loss in meaningless pursuits of one kind or another.

The work of education goes on at St Michael's Convent in a variety of forms, sustained by a daily round of worship and intercession. Many individuals and groups find their way here, for retreats and for a quiet venue for their own study, space, creativity or training. Residential accommodation is offered for these, as well as opportunities for people to come in the day, simply to have time apart and meet informally with the Sisters.

The convent is set in a large garden, offering a place for wandering and reflection. There are Friday lectures providing a forum for learning and discussion; the weekly D.E.E.E.P. S.E.A. (Dabble, Experiment, Explore, Express, Play—Serious Entertaining Action!) group affords opportunity for creativity. The annual Advent Meditation attracts a large number of people and the Sisters are able to raise money for charities other than themselves. There is a Peace and Justice noticeboard, and regular leaflets are available on this and other projects.

Some Sisters do voluntary work outside the convent. There are

Sustained by a daily round of worship and intercession

connections with local parishes, work with the Church for the Deaf, and pastoral visiting. Sisters also give talks, preach and lead Quiet Days, both outside and inside the house. All events are open to both women and men. Most meals are taken in silence with the Community. ∎

For a programme of events, please write to the Guest Sister, St Michael's Convent, 56 Ham Common, Richmond, Surrey TW10 7JH. Other enquiries may be made by: email (info@sistersofthechurch.org.uk); fax (020 8332 2927); phone (020 8940 8711).

Night

These prayers are by Jonny Baker, who works for the Church Mission Society developing mission and new ways of being church in the emerging culture. He lectures in mission and culture for the Centre for Youth Ministry, is a member of 'Grace', an alternative worship community, and has coordinated worship at Greenbelt for several years. He runs www.proost.co.uk, a company producing inspiring resources that fuel faith, and blogs at http://jonnybaker.blogs.com

Sunday

'If I say "Surely the darkness will hide me and the light become night around me," even the darkness will not be dark to you; the night will shine like the day for darkness is as light to you' (Psalm 139:11–12).

You are the Starlit Darkness
I come into your presence
unable to see a thing,
my eyes full of the busyness of the day,
pupils shrunk
from the brightness of the lights.
But I know you are here
So… I stand still, wait quietly,
stop rushing
breathe deeply, take time, slow down
And… gently, gradually
my eyes and heart adjust.
The stars that were there all along
come into view
Absence becomes presence
Blindness becomes sight
The darkness has become dazzling
You are here

You are a Pillar of Fire
At night Jesus prayed
Angels appeared
Visions were seen
Dreams were dreamed
Guidance was given.
God spoke
In my desert
In my uncertainty, in my confusion
In my darkness, in my night.
Guide my steps
Shine on the way I should go
Be my Pillar of Fire

Monday

'A wife of noble character who can find? … She gets up while it is still night; she provides food for her family and portions for her women servants… She sees that her trading is profitable, and her lamp does not go out at night' (Proverbs 31:10, 15, 18).

You are the Lamp
who does not go out at night
We pray for the night workers
who rise at crack of dawn,
who do night shifts
who work long hours in hospitals,
factories, studios, fields,
taxis, trains, and homes.
Be their Lamp
who does not go out at night

Tuesday

'By day the Lord went ahead of them in a pillar of cloud to guide them on their way and by night in a pillar of fire to give them light, so that they could travel by day or night' (Exodus 13:21).

Wednesday

'When you lie down, you will not be afraid; when you lie down, your sleep will be sweet' (Proverbs 3:24).

You are my Comfort and Duvet
In the night all my fears surface and
my worries loom large
as I replay worst case scenarios
in my head.
So… be with me tonight
May your presence comfort me,
Your love cast out fear
And I cast my worries on to you

I wrap my duvet tightly around me
to keep my warm, to keep me safe,
to keep me snug
Help me sleep sweetly
Be my Comfort
Be my Duvet

Thursday

'"I, Jesus, have sent my angel to give you this testimony for the churches. I am the Root and the Offspring of David, and the bright Morning Star"' (Revelation 22:16).

You are the Morning Star.
Thank you that you appear
at the darkest point of the night,
a glimmer of hope in the distance
heralding the coming dawn.
When the night is at its darkest,
appears the morning star,
a promise of the coming dawn.
Dreamers of the future,
living against the odds
bring newness to a weary land.
Seeds of hope—
Dare to sow seeds of hope

Friday

'The eye of the adulterer watches for dusk; he thinks, "No eye will see me"' (Job 24:15).

You are the Light of the World
Under cover of darkness
temptation rises
and people hide their deeds and faces
as they give in to her charms.
Help me resist temptation
in the things I hear
the places I go, the sights I see
the websites I visit, the words I say
the people I meet and the things I do.
Cleanse me from sin

Forgive me for where I have given in
and disobeyed you
Give me strength to resist Temptation.
You are the Light of the World
Shine in my darkness
Bring my deeds into your light

Saturday

'My eyes stay open through the watches of the night, that I may meditate on your promises' (Psalm 119:148).

You are my Promise
At night I slow down
It takes a while
but my breathing,
the blood rushing through my veins,
the things buzzing round my head,
the things I have done today,
and the things to do tomorrow,
gradually settle down,
and my heart stills.
Sometimes I just fall asleep
which is good and long
and deep and needed
But sometimes I savour the moment
and bring to my mind a verse
or a promise to turn over quietly
'I am with you'
'I will never leave you'
'As far as the heavens are above the
earth so great is your love for me'
'You are my child'
Thank you

Musings of a middle-aged mystic

Veronica Zundel is a journalist, author and contributor to 'New Daylight'. She has also written 'The Time of Our Lives' for BRF. She lives in north London.

In the midst of a breakdown 16 years ago, I became obsessed with a musical setting by Garth Hewitt of a poem called 'The Night' by the 17th-century poet Henry Vaughan. Starting with the story of Nicodemus visiting Jesus by night, the poem praises night as the time of rest, retreat and restoration:

Dear night!
this world's defeat;
The stop to busie fools;
care's check and curb;
The day of Spirits;
my soul's calm retreat
Which none disturb!

In my desperate state these words spoke to me as I longed for the escape of sleep, the only break from the fears that occupied my waking hours. Yet at the same time the poem terrified me with words such as these:

There is in God (some say)
A deep, but dazzling darkness;
As men here
Say it is late and dusky, because they
See not all clear
O for that night! where I in him
Might live invisible and dim.

These lines filled me with dread as I grappled with compulsions to harm myself in an irreversible way. So much of me longed for darkness, and the idea that God might still be in this darkness tempted me to act on my impulses. So this poem both attracted and repelled me, with its vision of night and darkness as the dwelling place of God.

> **Darkness** is just as much the home of God as light is

No wonder then that ancient people identified light with God

As well as a time of rest, night is, of course, a time when criminals operate, when wild beasts roam the darkness, a time of vulnerability and fears of the unknown. Before electric light, all human beings had to push back the darkness was a small circle of light created by a candle or oil lamp. Only the rich could afford chandeliers and multiple candlesticks to brighten their homes. Just before last Christmas our street had a power cut. It was a sobering experience suddenly to be plunged into darkness, to grope round the house for torches and candles, and to realize how dependent we are on electric current. We were very glad to have two gas fires to heat the house and a gas hob to cook on by torchlight. No wonder then that ancient people identified light with God: light enables us to function fully as human beings, to know and trust each other, to fulfil God's mandate to look after the earth.

The Bible tells us that 'God is light, and in him there is no darkness at all' (1 John 1:5, NRSV). Is Vaughan's vision of God in darkness, then, a heretical one? I think the answer is 'yes and no'. The psalmist, too, sees God hidden in darkness: 'If I say, "Surely the darkness shall cover me..." even the darkness is not dark to you... for darkness is as light to you' (Psalm 139:11–12). Perhaps it is like the effect of looking momentarily at the sun or a very bright light: because our eyes are not capable of adapting to such bright light, all we see for a few moments is darkness. Is that what Vaughan means by 'a deep but dazzling darkness'?

Now that I have recovered from the fears that haunted me during my breakdown, I find it comforting to know that darkness is just as much the home of God as light is. There is no night so dark that God's light is not hidden in it somewhere. 'I will give you the treasures of darkness,' God promises through the prophet Isaiah (45:3). Times of darkness will inevitably come in our lives, but the fact that we cannot see light at those times does not mean that no light exists. God's light shines even in darkness, 'and the darkness has not overcome it' (John 1:5). ∎

Visit the Quiet Spaces website **www.quietspaces.org.uk**

Do take a moment to visit the *Quiet Spaces* website (www.quietspaces.org.uk) and email us with your thoughts, perhaps sparked by what you have read in this issue.

In our next issue

For 2009 our *Quiet Spaces* themes will be Solitude, Community, Nation. In recent years there has been much debate about what 'community' and 'nation' signify and about what it means to belong to either of these groups. There are many implications for how we live out our faith and grow as disciples. Meanwhile solitude can be either positive or negative, depending on whether or not we feel we have a choice over our solitary state. Can God speak most clearly when we are alone?

Contact us at:

Quiet Spaces,
BRF,
15 The Chambers,
Vineyard, Abingdon
OX14 3FE
enquiries@brf.org.uk

QUIET SPACES SUBSCRIPTIONS

Quiet Spaces is published three times a year, in March, July and November. To take out a subscription, please complete this form, indicating the month in which you would like your subscription to begin.

☐ I would like to give a gift subscription (please complete both name and address sections below)

☐ I would like to take out a subscription myself (complete name and address details only once)

This completed coupon should be sent with appropriate payment to BRF. Alternatively, please write to us quoting your name, address, the subscription you would like for either yourself or a friend (with their name and address), the start date and credit card number, expiry date and signature if paying by credit card.

Gift subscription name _____

Gift subscription address _____

_____

_____ Postcode _____

Please send beginning with the next July / November / March issue: *(delete as applicable)*

(please tick box)   UK   SURFACE   AIR MAIL

Quiet Spaces   ☐ £16.95   ☐ £18.45   ☐ £20.85

Please complete the payment details below and send your coupon, with appropriate payment to: BRF, 15 The Chambers, Vineyard, Abingdon OX14 3FE.

Name _____

Address _____

_____

Postcode _____ Telephone Number _____

Email _____

☐ Please do not email me any information about BRF publications

Method of payment: ☐ Cheque ☐ Mastercard ☐ Visa ☐ Maestro ☐ Postal Order

Card no. ☐☐☐☐ ☐☐☐☐ ☐☐☐☐ ☐☐☐☐ ☐☐☐☐

Valid from ☐☐☐☐   Expires ☐☐☐☐   Issue no. of Maestro card ☐☐☐

Security Code ☐☐☐

Signature _____ Date ____ / ____ / ____

All orders must be accompanied by the appropriate payment.
Please make cheques payable to BRF

☐ Please do not send me further information about BRF publications

PROMO REF: QSNIGHT
BRF is a Registered Charity